Cello Stretching

Extended First Position

by Cassia Harvey

CHP243

©2014 by C. Harvey Publications All Rights Reserved.

6403 N. 6th Street
Philadelphia, PA 19126
www.charveypublications.com

Practice Suggestions for the Left Hand

1. Keep the wrist fairly straight to allow the arm to support the hand.
2. The thumb should be loosely balanced on the cello neck (never squeezing).
3. The thumb should generally be positioned under the 2nd finger.
4. Take frequent breaks to rest the hand and relieve any tension in the fingers.
5. Never force a stretch; the hand will become more flexible through gentle motions and repeated practice.
6. Stop if you feel any pain. Assess the tension in your hand or arm and try to relax specific muscles that might be causing trouble. Avoid back, neck, or arm positions that are contorted.
7. Practice this book after you have warmed up your hands (*Finger Exercises for the Cello, Book One*, CHP101 or *The Triplet Book for Cello, Part One*, CHP233).

Cello Stretching: Extended First Position

Stretching Back to a Flat

Cassia Harvey

In closed first position, the space between first and second fingers is a half step:

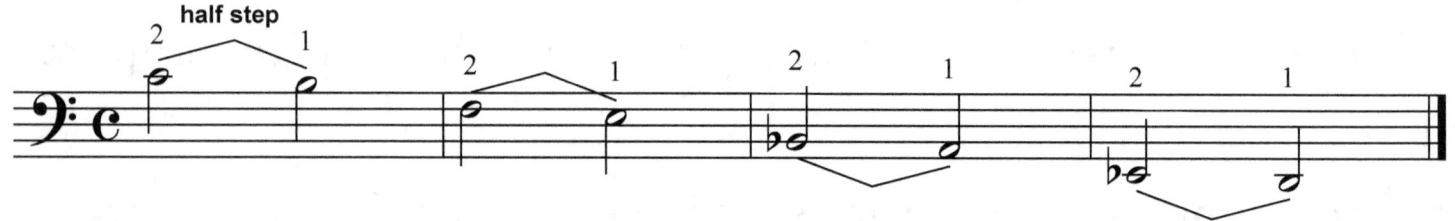

In order to reach some flats, the first finger extends back,
while the other fingers remain in first position:

The 2nd, 3rd, and 4th fingers are in closed (regular) first position

©2014 C. Harvey Publications All Rights Reserved.

Cello Stretching: Extended First Position

The Grey Goose

Trad., arr. Harvey

In the key of F major, every note B is flat.
Extend the first finger back to B♭ on the A string.

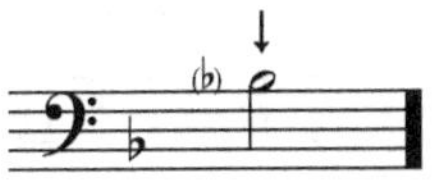

Au Clair de la Lune

Trad., arr. Harvey

©2014 C. Harvey Publications All Rights Reserved.

Stretching:

Hold every finger in place on the string until the next note is reached by the next finger.
By doing this, the hand will stretch instead of jump or shift.

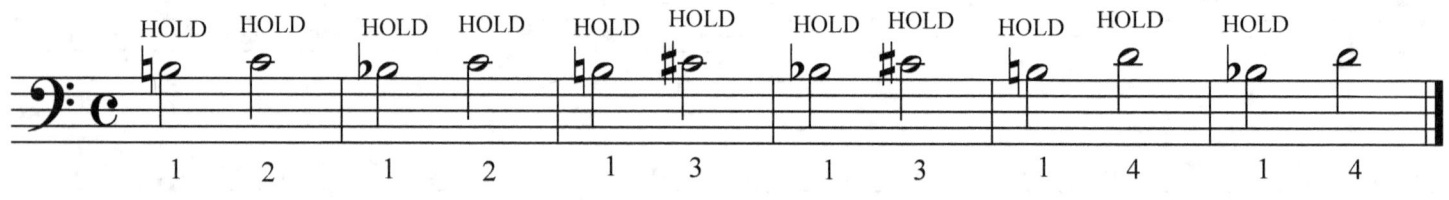

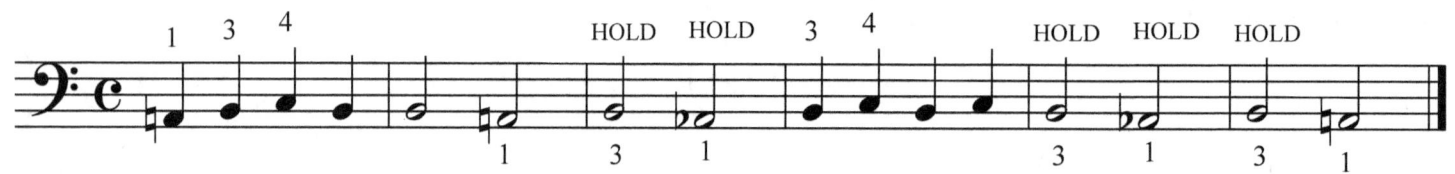

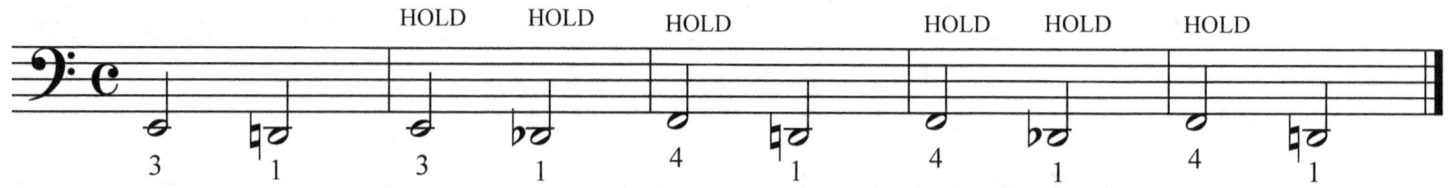

©2014 C. Harvey Publications All Rights Reserved.

Holding and Stretching Back to a Flat

Cello Stretching: Extended First Position

Groups of Three

Reaching Up to First Position from a Flat

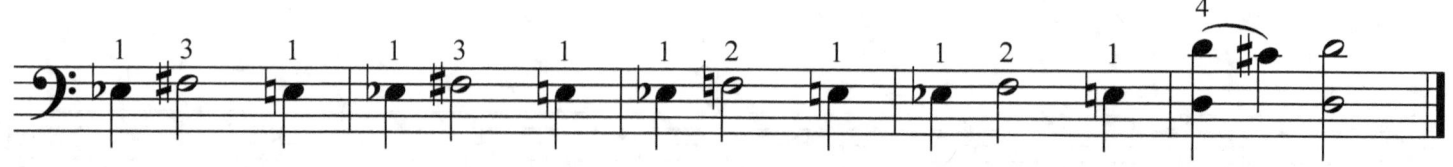

©2014 C. Harvey Publications All Rights Reserved.

Cello Stretching: Extended First Position

Before the Spring
Trad. Russian, arr. Harvey

In the key of E♭ major, all notes B, E, and A are flat.
Extend the first finger back to B♭ on the A string, E♭ on the D string, and A♭ on the G string.

Lullaby
Harvey

©2014 C. Harvey Publications All Rights Reserved.

Stretching Inside a Slur

Stretching Patterns No. 1

©2014 C. Harvey Publications All Rights Reserved.

Cello Stretching: Extended First Position

Four in a Bow

Stretching Patterns No. 2

©2014 C. Harvey Publications All Rights Reserved.

Cello Stretching: Extended First Position

Finger Exercise No. 1

Finger Exercise No. 2

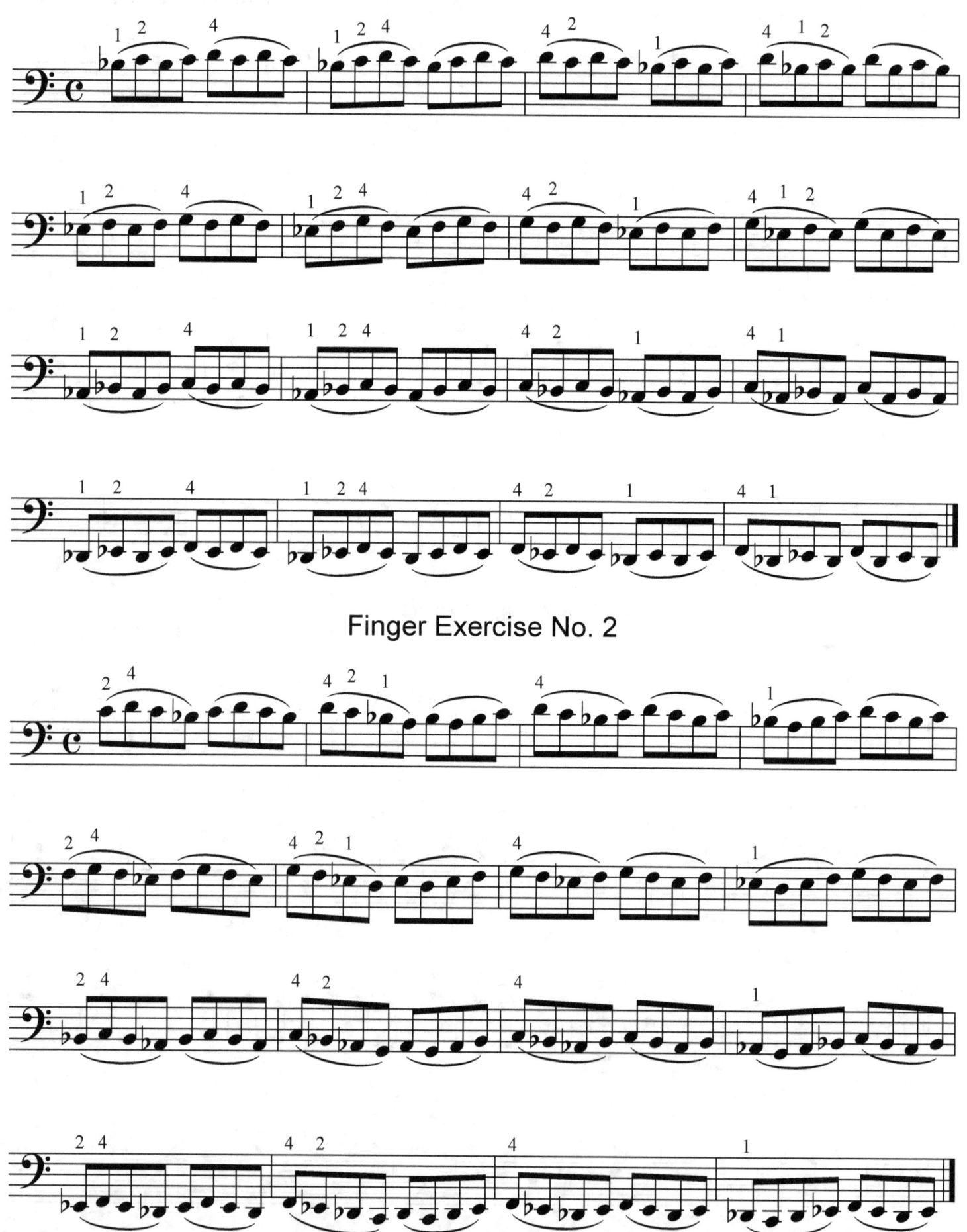

©2014 C. Harvey Publications All Rights Reserved.

Cello Stretching: Extended First Position

B♭ Study

Aria from 'Don Juan' With Variations

Mozart, arr. Harvey

Crossing From an Open String

Stretching Study No. 1

Stretching Study No. 2

Stretching Study No. 3

Stretching Study No. 4

©2014 C. Harvey Publications All Rights Reserved.

Cello Stretching: Extended First Position

Girofle Girofla

Trad. French, arr. Harvey

Folk Song

Trad. Russian, arr. Harvey

©2014 C. Harvey Publications All Rights Reserved.

Cello Stretching: Extended First Position

Le Furet du Bois Joli

Trad. French, arr. Harvey

Theme from 1812 Overture

Tchaikovsky, arr. Harvey

©2014 C. Harvey Publications All Rights Reserved.

Across Strings With 1st and 4th Fingers

Stretching Study No. 7

Stretching Study No. 8

Stretching Study No. 9

©2014 C. Harvey Publications All Rights Reserved.

Cello Stretching: Extended First Position

Pop Goes the Weasel
Trad. American, arr. Harvey

Song of Shores
Trad. Russian, arr. Harvey

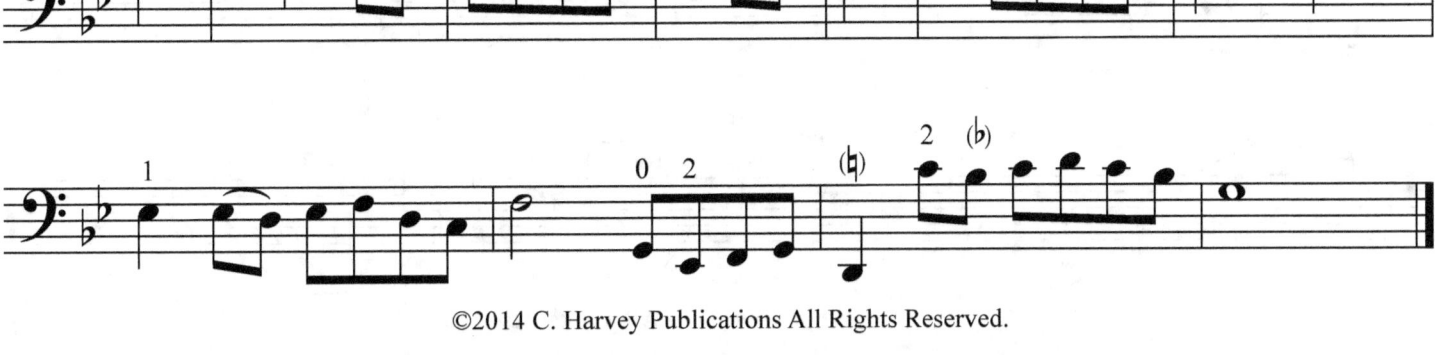

©2014 C. Harvey Publications All Rights Reserved.

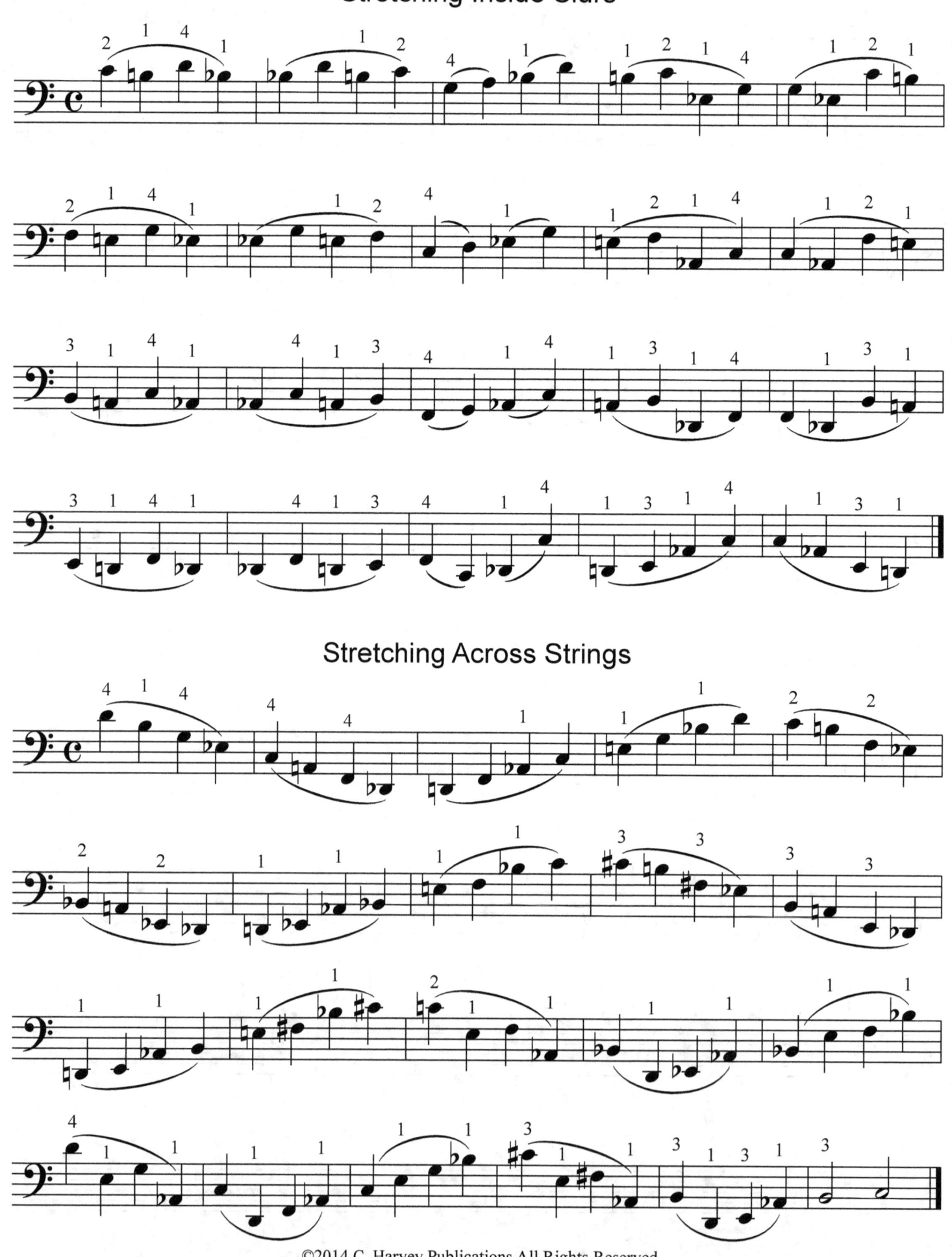

Cello Stretching: Extended First Position

Little Tommy Tucker
Trad. English, arr. Harvey

Folk Song
Trad. Ukranian, arr. Harvey

©2014 C. Harvey Publications All Rights Reserved.

Switching to Extended Position Across Strings

Stretching Exercise No. 10

Stretching Exercise No. 11

©2014 C. Harvey Publications All Rights Reserved.

Cello Stretching: Extended First Position

La Polichinelle
Trad. French, arr. Harvey

Go to Sleep
Trad. American, arr. Harvey

©2014 C. Harvey Publications All Rights Reserved.

Stretching Forward to a Sharp

The typical hand position on the cello reaches
one whole and one half step from 1st to 4th finger:

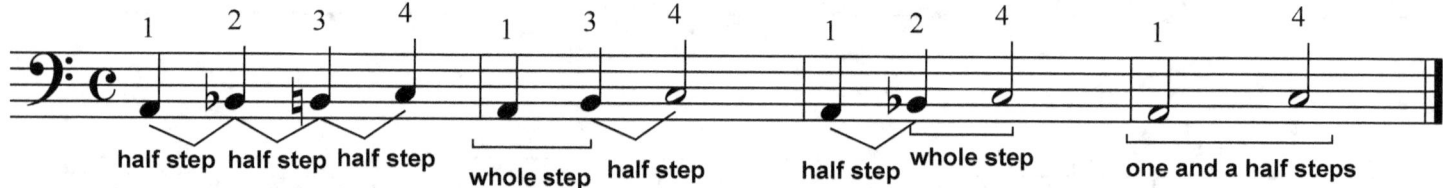

To reach two whole steps, the fingers must extend. This extension most often occurs between
the 1st and 2nd fingers, as these are usually the most capable fingers for stretching.

Extend the hand forward by reaching to put 2nd finger where 3rd finger would usually go.
At the same time, **slide the thumb up on the neck to be directly under the extended 2nd finger.**

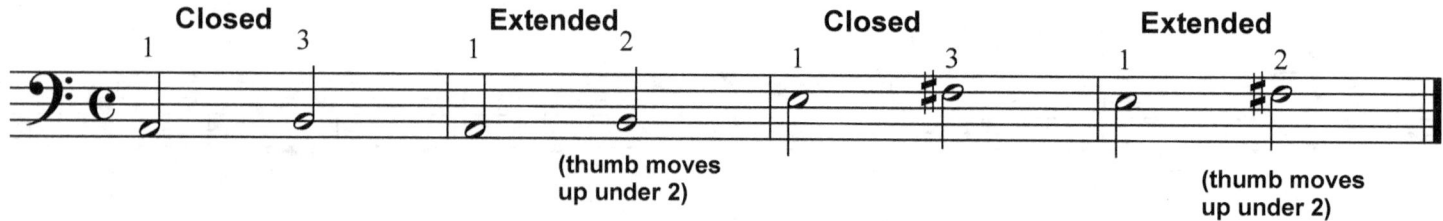

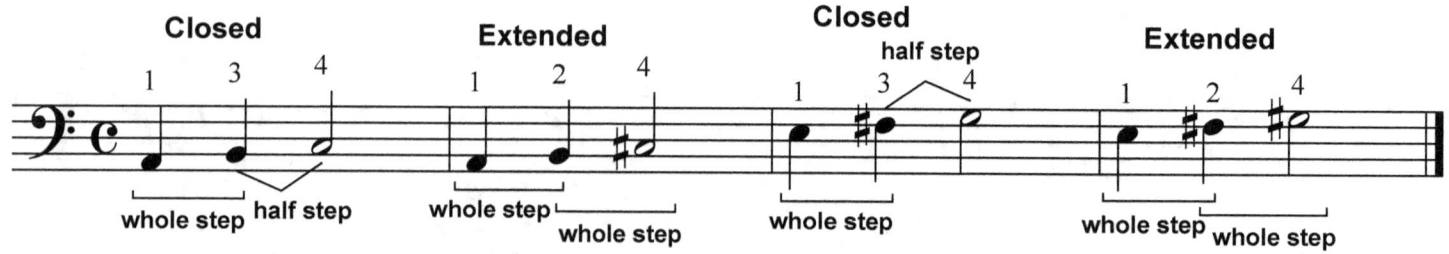

**Don't forget to slide your thumb up on
the neck to be under the 2nd finger!**

©2014 C. Harvey Publications All Rights Reserved.

Cello Stretching: Extended First Position

©2014 C. Harvey Publications All Rights Reserved.

Stretching

A string

D string

G string

C string

©2014 C. Harvey Publications All Rights Reserved.

Stretching into Extended Position

In and Out of Extended Position

©2014 C. Harvey Publications All Rights Reserved.

Cello Stretching: Extended First Position

Sur le pont d'Avingnon

Trad. French, arr. Harvey

Down the River

Trad. Chantey, arr. Harvey

©2014 C. Harvey Publications All Rights Reserved.

Stretching to 4th Finger

Stretching

Note: do not stretch at all between 2nd and 4th fingers.

Don't forget to slide your thumb up on the neck to be under the 2nd finger!

Groups of Three Notes

©2014 C. Harvey Publications All Rights Reserved.

Cello Stretching: Extended First Position

Morning Song
Mason, arr. Harvey

Finlandia
Sibelius, arr. Harvey

©2014 C. Harvey Publications All Rights Reserved.

Half Steps Between 2nd, 3rd, and 4th Fingers

Double Stops and Stretching

Cello Stretching: Extended First Position

Fais Dodo, Colas
Trad. French, arr. Harvey

Folk Tune
Trad. Armenian, arr. Harvey

©2014 C. Harvey Publications All Rights Reserved.

Cello Stretching: Extended First Position

Johnny Shoemaker

Trad. American, arr. Harvey

Let's Go Walking

Gaudette, arr. Harvey

©2014 C. Harvey Publications All Rights Reserved.

Stretching Finger Exercise No. 1

Stretching Finger Exercise No. 2

©2014 C. Harvey Publications All Rights Reserved.

Cello Stretching: Extended First Position

Walking with the Wagons
Harvey

La Mere Michel
Trad. French, arr. Harvey

Sliding into Extended Position

Opening the Hand Into Extended Position

(thumb moves up under 2)

Cello Stretching: Extended First Position   43

Song

Brahms, arr. Harvey

The Month of Showers

Hartford, arr. Harvey

©2014 C. Harvey Publications All Rights Reserved.

Stretching Finger Exercise No. 3

Trad., arr. Harvey

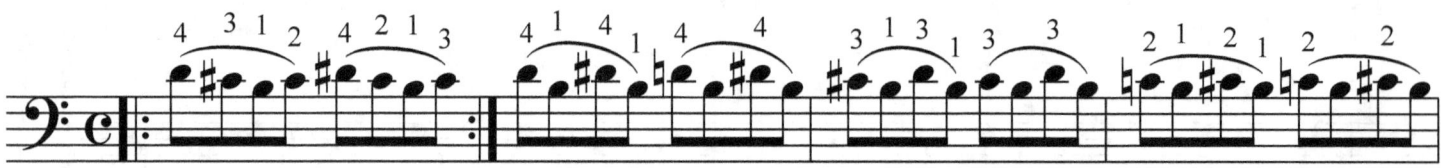

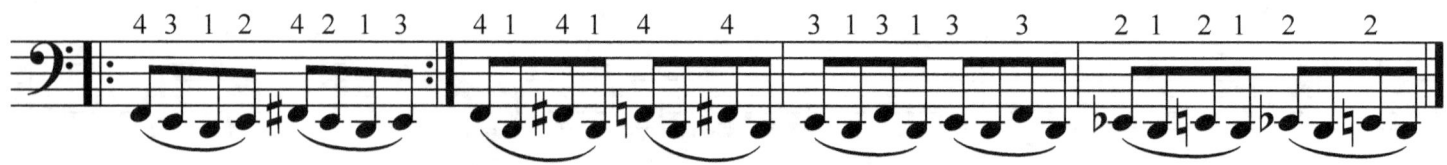

Stretching Finger Exercise No. 4

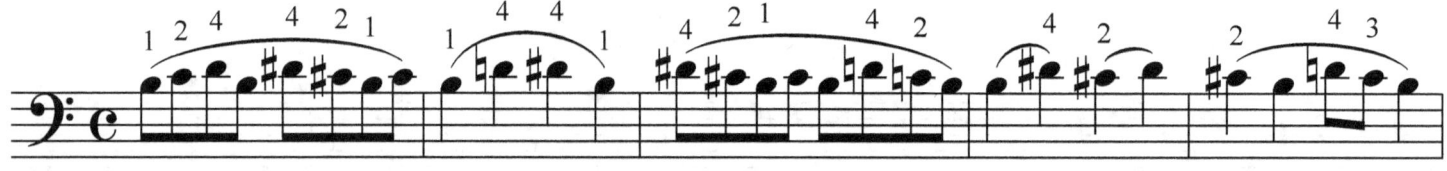

©2014 C. Harvey Publications All Rights Reserved.

Cello Stretching: Extended First Position

Sonatina
Beethoven, arr. Harvey

Mother Mousehawk's Lullaby
Trad. Eskimo, arr. Harvey

©2014 C. Harvey Publications All Rights Reserved.

46 Stretching

Arpeggio Patterns

More Across Strings

All the Pretty Little Horses
Trad. American, arr. Harvey

©2014 C. Harvey Publications All Rights Reserved.

Cello Stretching: Extended First Position

La Czarine
Ganne, arr. Harvey

A Major Study

Light Cavalry Overture
von Suppe, arr. Harvey

©2014 C. Harvey Publications All Rights Reserved.

Extending Across Strings

More Extending Across Strings

Cello Stretching: Extended First Position

Varvisa
Mozart, arr. Harvey

The Ebullient Dancers
Trad. Spanish, arr. Harvey

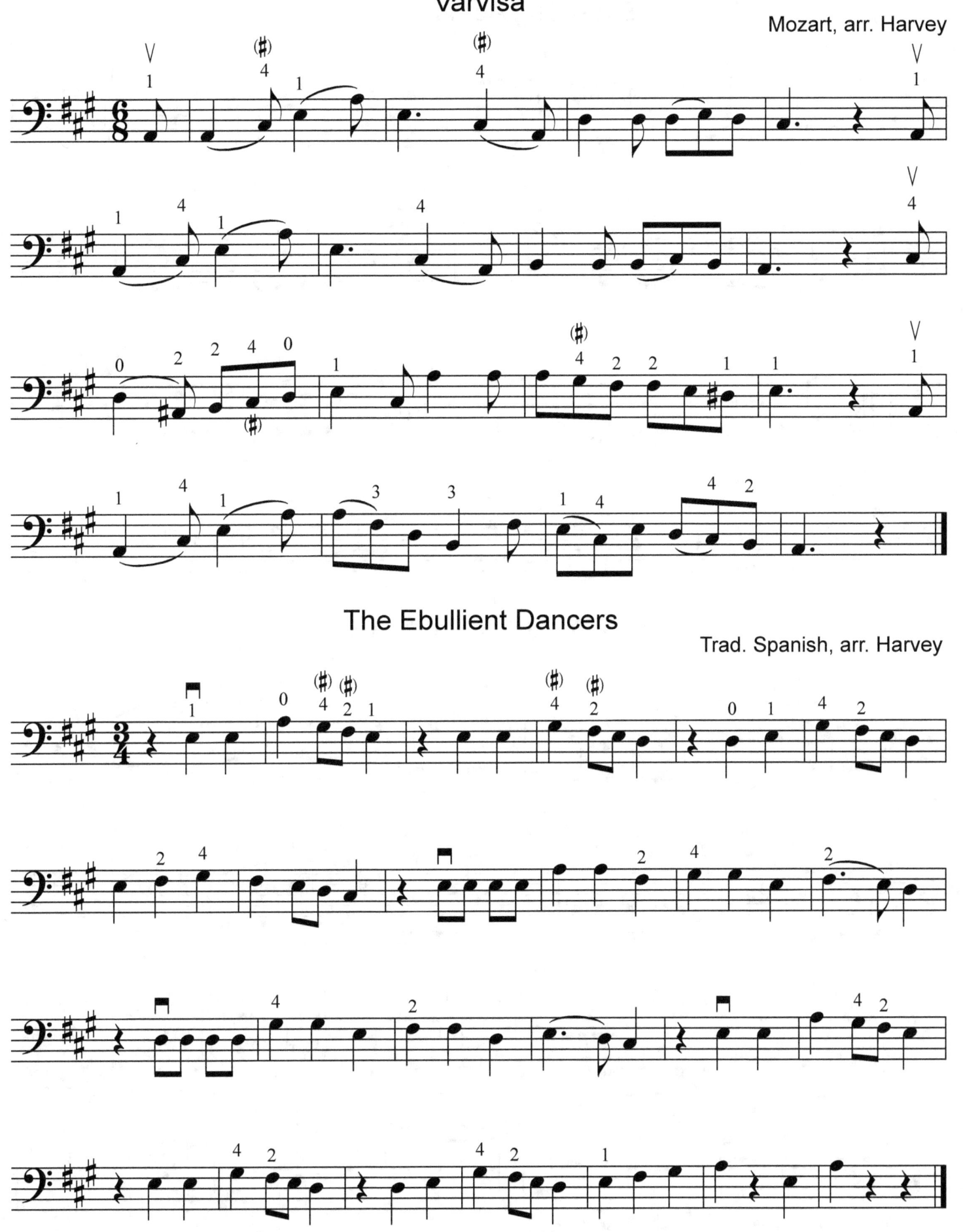

©2014 C. Harvey Publications All Rights Reserved.

Extending Across Strings

Extending to 4th Finger

Cello Stretching: Extended First Position

Pingsthymn
Bach, arr. Harvey

March
Harvey

©2014 C. Harvey Publications All Rights Reserved.

Switching Between Extended Positions

Extended Positions Study No. 1

Cello Stretching: Extended First Position

Theme from Symphony No. 7

Beethoven, arr. Harvey

Cello Stretching: Extended First Position 59

La Chasse
Biehl, arr. Harvey

Waltz No. 1
Brahms, arr. Harvey

©2014 C. Harvey Publications All Rights Reserved.

Finger Exercise No. 3

Slurred Stretching

Cello Stretching: Extended First Position

Tutu Maramba

Trad. Brazilian, arr. Harvey

Theme from Lucia di Lammermoor

Donizetti, arr. Harvey

©2014 C. Harvey Publications All Rights Reserved.

Cello Stretching: Extended First Position

Moderato

Stift, arr. Harvey

6 in a Bow

Extended Positions Study No. 2

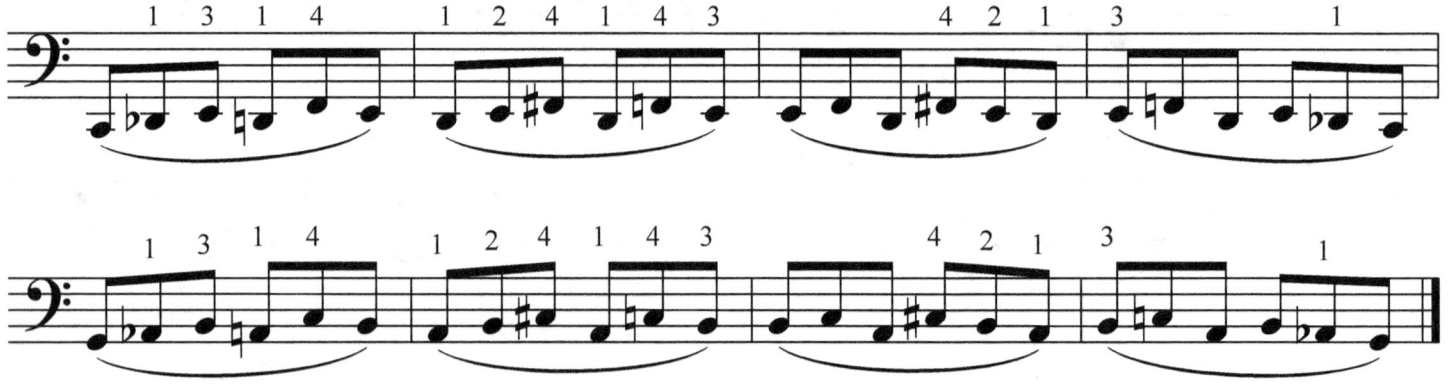

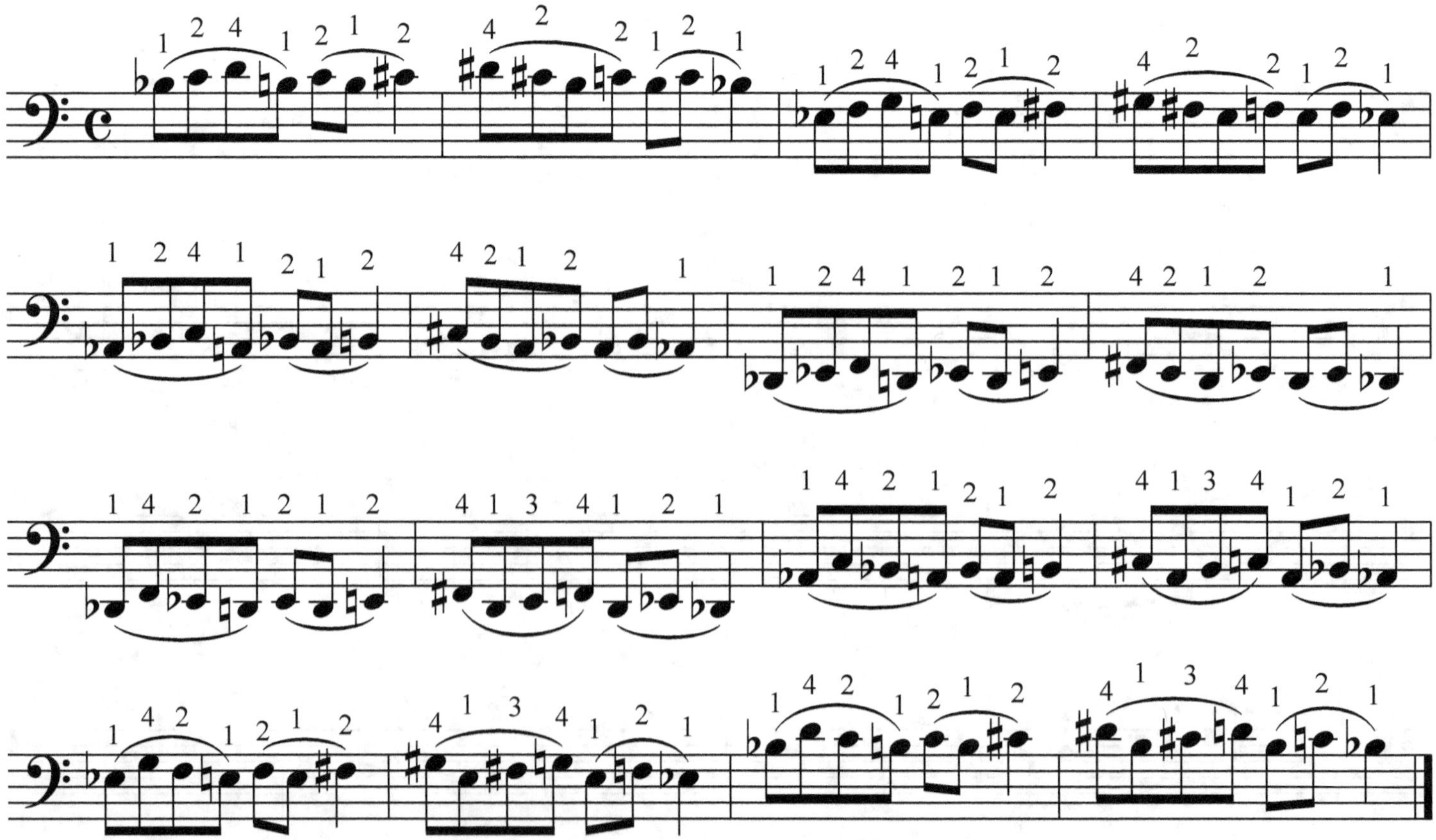

Cello Stretching: Extended First Position

Country Song
Trad. Swedish, arr. Harvey

As a Shepherdess
Bellman, arr. Harvey

©2014 C. Harvey Publications All Rights Reserved.

Study No. 3: Shifting Into Extended Positions

Sliding into Extended Positions

(thumb moves up under 2)

(thumb moves up under 2)

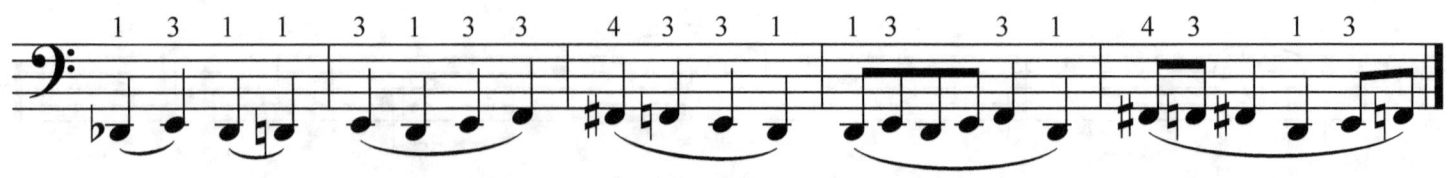

©2014 C. Harvey Publications All Rights Reserved.

Cello Stretching: Extended First Position

E Major Exercise

Trolls
Harvey

©2014 C. Harvey Publications All Rights Reserved.

Double Stops

(thumb moves up under 2)

(thumb moves up under 2)

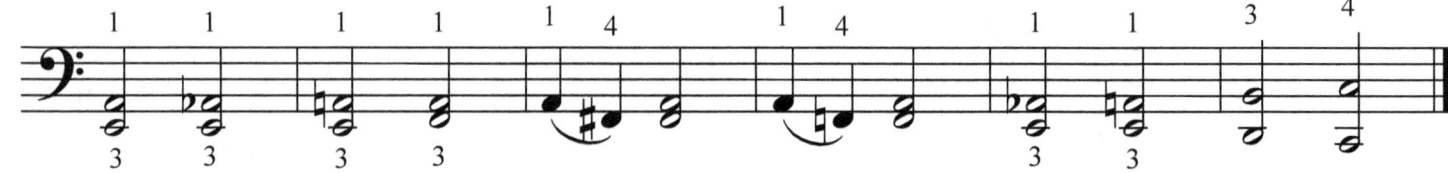

Extended Positions Study No. 4

©2014 C. Harvey Publications All Rights Reserved.

Cello Stretching: Extended First Position

Concerto Theme

Telemann, arr. Harvey

Variations on "The Woman and the Peddler"

Trad., arr. Harvey

©2014 C. Harvey Publications All Rights Reserved.

A Major Study

Sliding into Extended Positions

L'Alphabet de Musique

Schickhardt, arr. Harvey

©2014 C. Harvey Publications All Rights Reserved.

Cello Stretching: Extended First Position

Extended Positions Study No. 5

Extended Positions Study No. 6

Cello Stretching: Extended First Position

Andante

Stift, arr. Harvey

©2014 C. Harvey Publications All Rights Reserved.

Cello Stretching: Extended First Position

Grieg Exercise

In the Hall of the Mountain King

Grieg, arr. Harvey

©2014 C. Harvey Publications All Rights Reserved.

Extended Positions Study No. 9

Extended Positions Study No. 10

Cello Stretching: Extended First Position

Bourree
Bach, arr. Harvey

Cielito Lindo
Trad. Mexican, arr. Harvey

©2014 C. Harvey Publications All Rights Reserved.

Extended Positions Study No. 11

Sliding Into Extended Positions

Cello Stretching: Extended First Position

Extended Positions Study No. 12

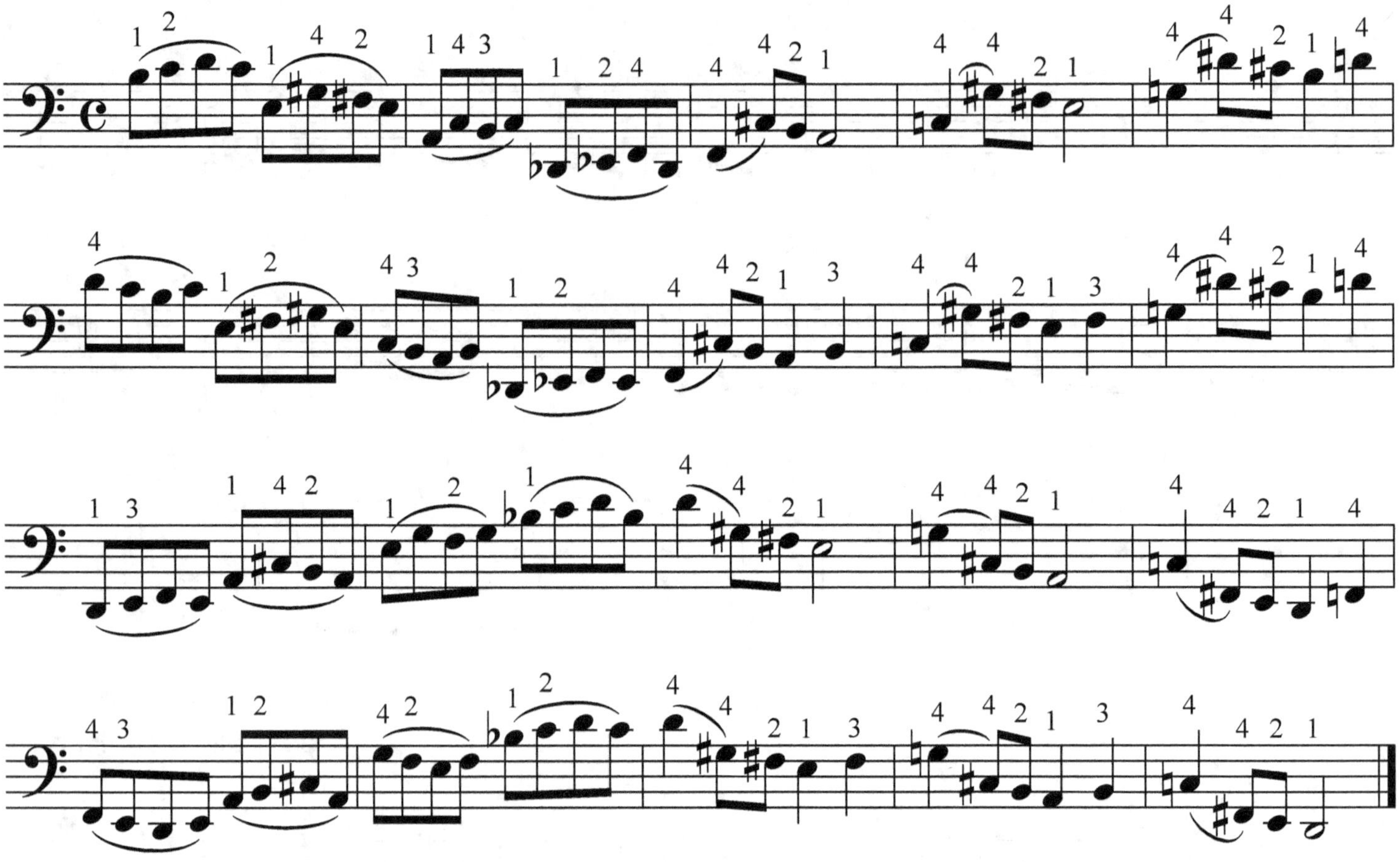

Extended Positions Study No. 13

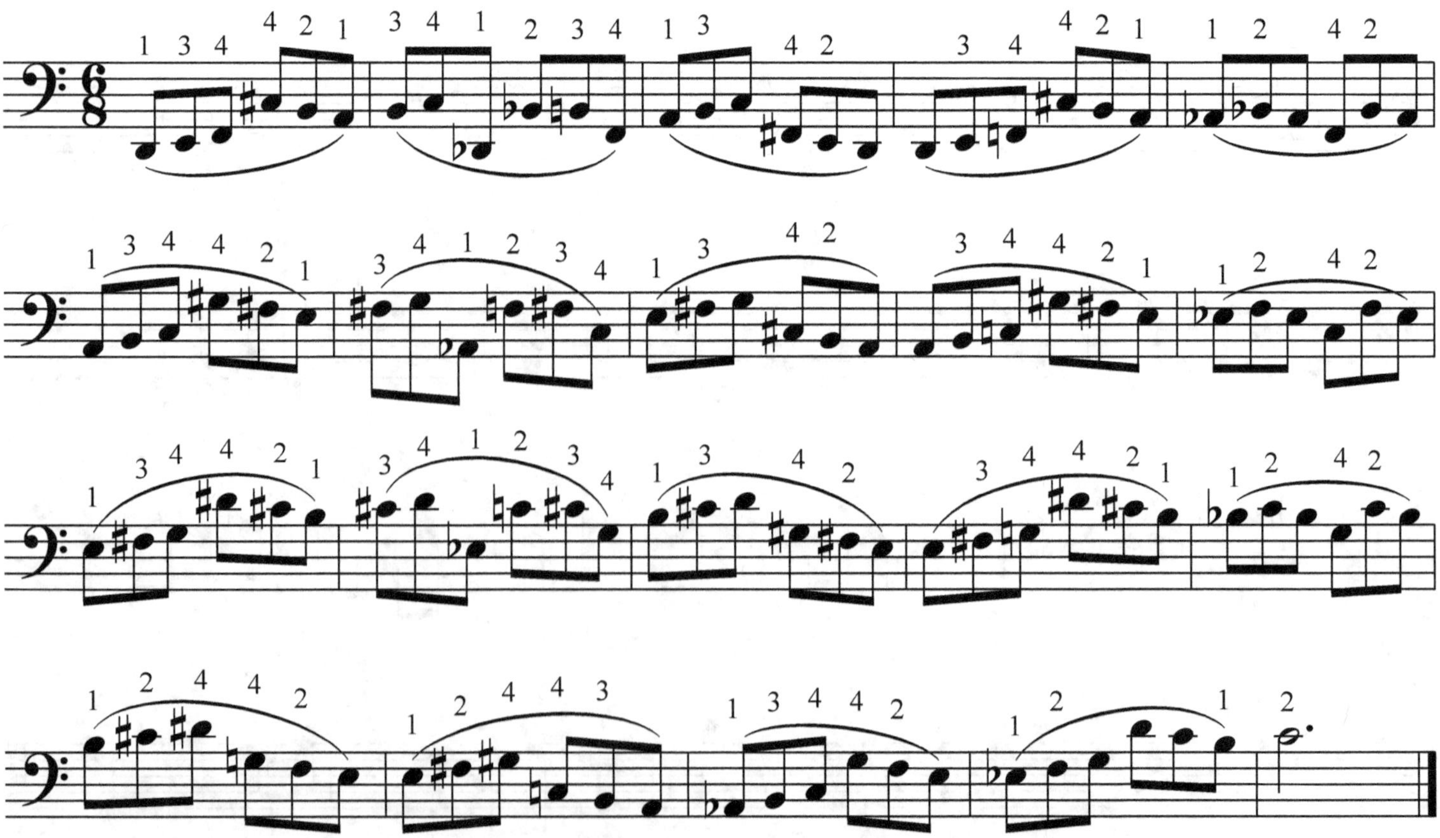

©2014 C. Harvey Publications All Rights Reserved.

Cello Stretching: Extended First Position

Gavotte

Bach, arr. Harvey

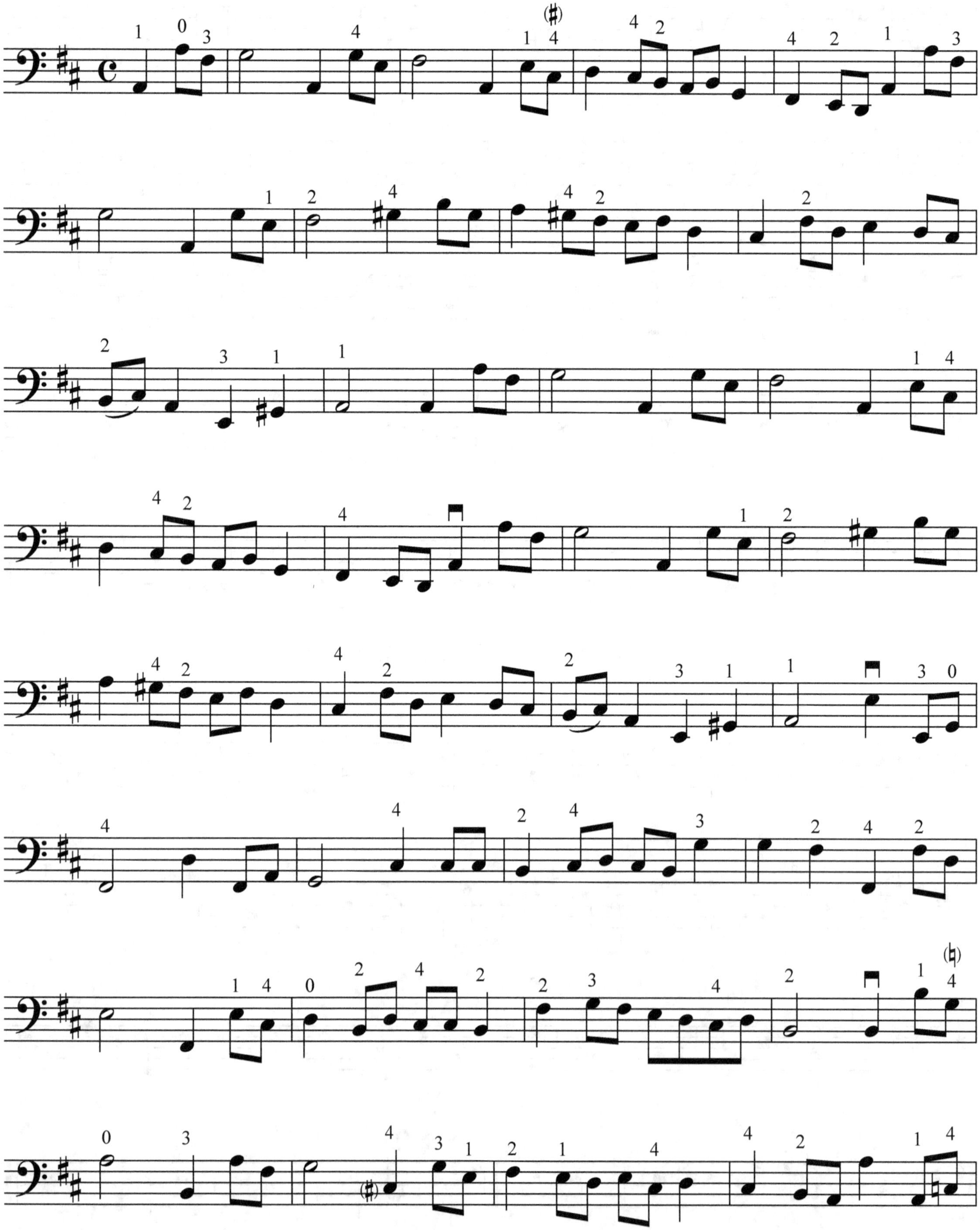

©2014 C. Harvey Publications All Rights Reserved.

Cello Stretching: Extended First Position

Also available from www.charveypublications.com: CHP363
The Romberg Cello Sonata in E Minor Practice Edition

Preparatory Exercises for Movement One

1. Fourth Position Notes and Bowing
Measures 1-3

©2020 C. Harvey Publications   All Rights Reserved.

www.ingramcontent.com/pod-product-compliance
Lightning Source LLC
Chambersburg PA
CBHW051421070526
44584CB00023B/3525